ACTIVE SCIENCE

Keep It
Afloat!

This edition 2004

First published in 1993 by
Franklin Watts
96 Leonard Street
London EC2A 4XD

Franklin Watts Australia
45-51 Huntley Street
Alexandria NSW 2015

Editorial planning: Serpentine Editorial
Scientific consultant: Dr. J.J.M.Rowe

Designed by the R & B Partnership
Illustrator: David Anstey
Photography: Peter Millard

Additional photographs:
Chris Fairclough Colour Library 10, 12;
ZEFA 11, 14, 20, 22, 29, 30 (top), 31 (top);
GI Bernard/NHPA 30 (bottom).

A CIP catalogue record for this book is
available from the British Library

ISBN 0 7496 5621 2

Printed in Malasyia

ACTIVE SCIENCE

Keep It Afloat!

Julian Rowe
and Molly Perham

W

FRANKLIN WATTS
LONDON•SYDNEY

Contents

FIFE COUNCIL SCHOOLS	
746153	
PETERS	05-Dec-06
J532	£5.99
JHOW	AD

 SAFETY WARNING
Activities marked with this symbol require the presence and
help of an adult. Plastic should always be used instead of glass.
Take special care near water.

Floaters and sinkers

This girl is sailing her boat on the pool.
It floats on the water.
A puff of wind fills
the sail and takes
the boat to the
other side.

Have you ever thrown a pebble into a pool?
It sinks straight to the bottom.
All you see is a circle of ripples
on the surface of the pool.

Test it out

This boy is collecting all kinds of things to test. Some of them are natural objects such as a lemon, shells, a cork and a fir-cone. Others are household objects.

Which things float and which sink? How can you find out?

You can use a plastic fish tank or large
bowl to test things. See how the marbles
and the shells have sunk to the bottom.
Which things are floating on the top?

The lemon floats because
the peel contains tiny
pockets of air. Why does
the peeled lemon sink?

Boats afloat

Inside the hull of a sailing dinghy there are hollow spaces filled with air. These stop the dinghy sinking if it is blown over, or capsizes.

A giant passenger liner is very heavy.
It weighs as much as a big building.

But it floats because, like the dinghy,
its hull is hollow and contains air.

Cargo ships

This ship carries thousands of tonnes of cargo. The heavy containers are carefully loaded so that the boat does not tip over and sink.

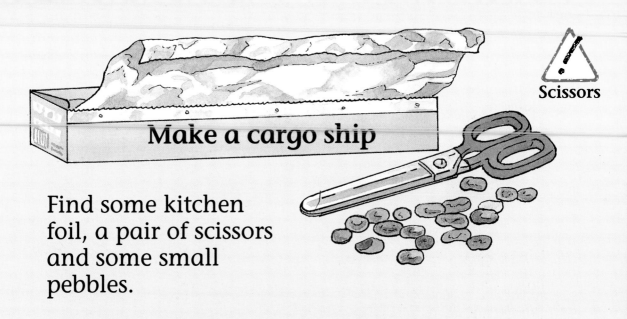

Make a cargo ship

Find some kitchen foil, a pair of scissors and some small pebbles.

Cut a piece of foil the size of this page. Bend up the edges on each side.

Fold the corners so that water cannot get in.

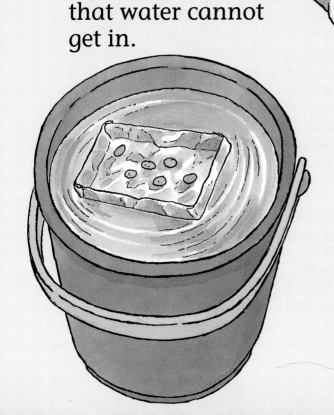

Float your boat in a bucket full of water. Now try loading it with pebbles. What happens if you put them all in one corner?

Water pushes back

Have you ever paddled an inflatable boat?
Why do you think it floats so easily in
the water?

When you push the paddle through the
water, can you feel the water pushing back?

This big ball is full of air. It floats right on top of the water. If you try to sink it, you can feel the water pushing back.

Learning to swim

Have you ever played with a beach ball in the water?

If you hold on to the ball, it will keep you afloat, or buoyant.

This girl is learning to swim.
Her armbands are full of air.
They are called buoyancy aids.

Under the water

Plants that live under the water have pockets of air inside them. These keep the plants floating in the water.

Fish have their own buoyancy aid, called a swim bladder, inside their bodies. They can control the amount of air in the swim bladder. This allows them to float higher or lower in the water.

Submarines

A submarine rises up and sinks down in the water like a fish.

When it dives, air is pumped out of its buoyancy tanks and water comes in. When the water is blown out, the submarine rises.

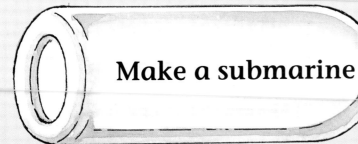

Make a submarine

Find a plastic bottle, a piece of
plastic tubing and some plasticine.

Make a hole in the
bottom of the bottle.
Cover it with
plasticine.

Make a hole in the cap.
Push the piece of
plastic tubing
through it.

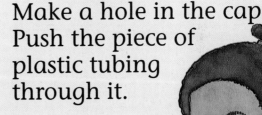

Fill the bottle with water.
Screw the cap back on.

Put your submarine
under water in a
large bowl or tank.
Remove the plasticine.

Now blow down the tube
and watch your submarine rise to the surface.

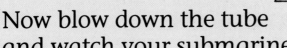

Lighter than water

Some things float because they are lighter than water. Ice is lighter than water.

Huge icebergs float in the seas around the North Pole.

Make an iceberg

Find an empty yoghurt pot. Fill it with water and put it in the freezer.

When the water has frozen, hold the yoghurt pot under a running tap until the ice inside loosens. Take out the block of ice.

Put your iceberg in a bowl of water. How much is under the water?

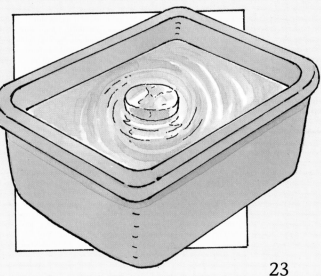

Oil and water

Oil is lighter than water.
It spreads out on the
surface of the water.
When it rains, you can
see oily patterns in
puddles on the street.

If a tanker spills some oil at sea, the oil
spreads far and wide.
It does not mix with the water.

Make oily pictures

White spirit

Find some oil paints, white spirit, an oven tray, some thick paper and an old fork.

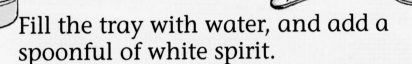

Fill the tray with water, and add a spoonful of white spirit.

Put some drops of oil paint onto the water.

Stir the colours around with the fork to make a pattern.

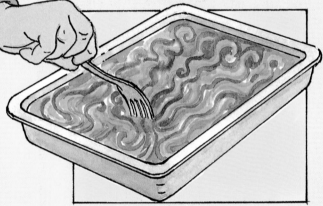

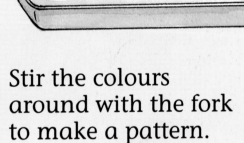

Carefully lay the piece of paper flat on the water. Lift the paper quickly and let the water drip off. Pin your picture up to dry.

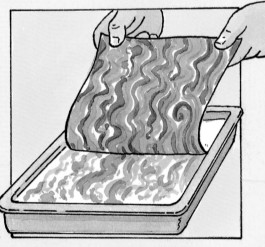

Soapy water

Oil mixes with water if detergent is added. These children are washing greasy plates using a detergent.

When seabirds swim into oily water, the oil sticks to their feathers. The oil can be removed with a detergent, which is then washed away.

Mixing oil and water

Find a clean empty bottle with a screw cap, some washing-up liquid and some cooking oil.

Put some oil in the bottle.

Half fill the bottle with water. See how the oil rises to the top.

Add a few drops of washing-up liquid.

Now screw the cap onto the bottle and give it a good shake.
What has happened to the oil?

Floating on air

Just as some liquids are lighter than water, some gases are lighter than air. The boy is holding balloons filled with helium gas. Helium is lighter than air, so the balloons float.

Hot-air balloons float because the warm air inside them is lighter than the cold air outside.

Think about... floating

Ducks spend most of their day
floating on water. The quills of their feathers
are hollow and contain air.

Giant coconuts float
for hundreds of
miles from one
island to another in
the Pacific Ocean.
These seeds then grow
into new trees.

What is the easiest way to move heavy logs? In Canada great rafts of logs are pulled by tug-boat to the sawmill.

Have you ever put a message in a bottle? If you throw it into the ocean, it could float all the way to another country.